This Book Belongs To:

____

Color Test Page

fuck off
I'm coloring

Value yourself
and others

SOMETIMES
LIFE SUCK

Positive thinking
makes it happen

Adopt the pace of
nature: her secret
is patience.
- Ralph Waldo Emerson

Love yourself
and others

Things i want to
say at work
but can't

JUST
Breathe

The best bridge between despair and hope is a good night's sleep.
E. Joseph Cossman

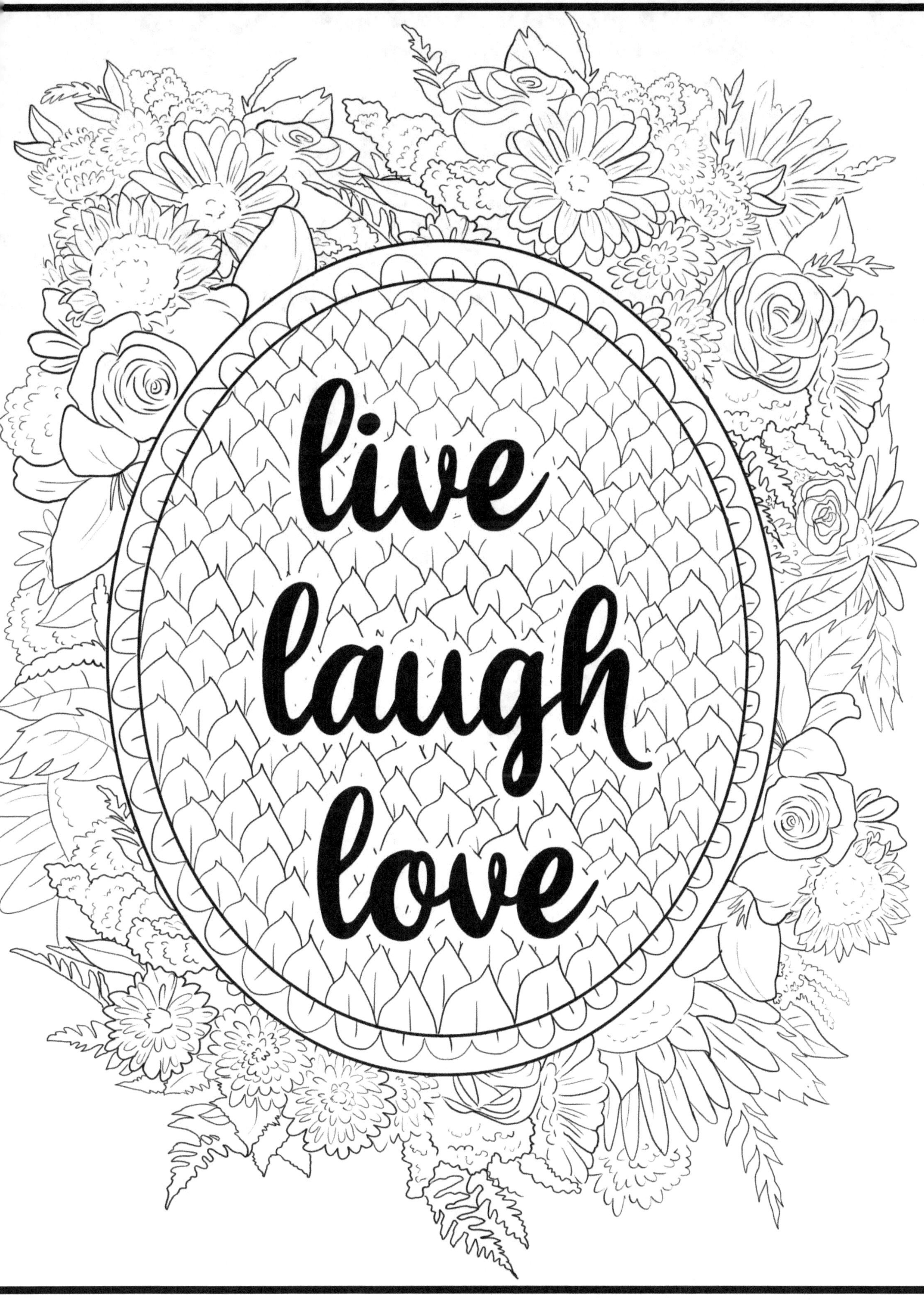
live
laugh
love

WHEN THE
flower blooms,
the bees
COME UNINVITED.
- Ramakrishna

Never
fucking
give up

Every day is
a good
day

I can't
fix stupid

Create
your
own
Reality

Life
IS
LIKE
A
ROAD
trip
Enjoy each day
BUT
don't carry
too much
BAGGAGE

As the sun shines both on the cedar tree and the smallest flower, so the Divine sun illumines each soul.
Therese of Lisieux

INHALE THE
GOOD SHIT
EXHALE THE
BULLSHIT

INHALE THE
GOOD SHIT
EXHALE THE
BULLSHIT

Open your
heart to your dreams

Be the
BEST
fuck the
rest

Life
IS LIKE A
Cup of Tea
IT'S ALL IN HOW YOU
make it

cheer the
fuck up

calm the
fuck down

Harmony
brings health
and happiness

Life
IS
LIKE
A
THORNY
but
Beautiful